A little bit of

GRATITUDE

Goes a long way

by Julie Ann Sullivan

Published by LNE Press, Pittsburgh, PA

Copyright © 2012 by Julie Ann Sullivan
4th printing
ISBN 9781483972091

How to Use This Book

This book is designed to allow the reader the opportunity to expand their ability to be grateful. There are 30 different areas to be grateful for in these pages. You could choose to do one a day for a month and on the 31st day make up your own. Or, you could choose to take one aspect and work on that for a period of time. No matter how you choose to do the work within these pages, there will always be something new for you to experience each time you return. Don't be fooled by thinking each page can only be a time to learn once. The same page can inspire you in new ways many times over. That is the beauty of being an ever-changing human.

So choose your own way and try something new. Be grateful to yourself that you are willing to become anew.

Thank you, Beth Caldwell. Over lunch, while discussing my newfound appreciation for *Gratitude*, you came up with the idea for this book and I ran with it. You gave me the opportunity to share my feelings about the importance of *Gratitude* to Pittsburgh Professional Women and promote this concept. It's like you opened the floodgates and I rushed on through to make this idea a reality.

To my readers,
In 2011, I dedicated my entire year to *Gratitude*. At that time, I had a very strong feeling that if I created more *Gratitude* in my life, my attitude towards everything would be different. I kept a daily journal and worked on being increasingly aware of the gifts in my life. It started with being joyful just to wake up every day and grew to my appreciating the simple wonders of life: the new bloom of a flower, the blue sky, a stranger's smile, and the many fortuitous moments that happen every day. These special moments, gifts if you will, were not new in my life, but I was now making room to be able to truly experience them. My assumption was right. This abundance of new joys has made a profound difference in my life. Even events that once threw me off course are now seen with a more positive attitude.

Increased *Gratitude* has given me more joy, less stress and an ever-expanding peaceful heart. My hope is that this book will reveal to you more ways to increase the peace and joy in your life as well.

Julie Ann

I am thankful for this opportunity to share.

What a gift to have you here to share in my thoughts. The mere fact that you have chosen to be a part of this shows your desire to want more Gratitude in your life. Good for you!

Don't forget to celebrate the times that you are good to yourself and the times that you accomplish anything. Don't spend too much time being interested in what you don't get done, instead of being grateful for being successful. It might be landing a big job, or playing with your child, or cleaning the oven. They are all accomplishments to celebrate. Write down what you did today that you forgot to celebrate.

_____

_____

_____

_____

_____

I'm thankful for nature and all of its beauty.

Each day there is a new part of nature to explore. Look to see a flower in bloom, the color of a leaf, or listen to the song of a bird. As the seasons change, these attributes change as well. So, with each new day there is an abundance of nature to appreciate.

List what you have learned today about the Earth that surrounds you. With each aspect you learn, that is one more reason to have Gratitude.

_____

_____

_____

_____

_____

_____

I am thankful for the senses I possess.

Each sense I have has given me a different opportunity to experience the life around me. As I become more attuned to my sight, hearing, smell, taste and sense of touch, wonders about my universe reveal themselves to me. Even the wind across my skin is an event I can appreciate.

Pick one of the five senses to be hyper-aware of today. Write what your increased awareness allows you to notice that you have not experienced before.

_____

_____

_____

_____

_____

_____

I am thankful that this world is filled with children.

The ability to watch a child enjoy life gives me the chance to see life through their perspective. Their sense of play reminds me how important it is to have that feeling of freedom until my last breath.

Do something *childlike* today and write about how it made you feel.

_____

_____

_____

_____

_____

_____

I am thankful for the trees.

Their shade cools my home and gives
me refuge from the elements. Their
roots stop the earth from moving in a
destructive way. Their leaves,
although they may be plentiful, give
me work to do, time to share, and the
ability to create a pile to jump in.

The beauty of trees changes with the seasons. You can witness birth in the spring, shade in the summer, color in the fall and the beauty of nakedness in the winter. What is going on in your world? Write about what the trees are doing in your neighborhood today.

_____

_____

_____

_____

_____

I am thankful for sleep.

It is my responsibility to create an atmosphere where I can get adequate restful sleep. When I do this and climb into the sanctuary of my bed, I am thankful not only for the opportunity, but for the bed I have to sleep in as well, with all its accoutrements.

Whether it is an extra 10 minutes in the morning, naps, or a good night's sleep, create a space to really relax and wash away the cares of the day. Create an atmosphere so you can succumb to a deep rest. When you do, how is it different when you return to your daily routine? Write it here to remind yourself in the future.

_____

_____

_____

_____

_____

_____

I am thankful for my life.

The mere idea that I am alive today is astounding. It is no small wonder. Focusing on the precious gift I have in just being alive showers my day with Gratitude.

Wake up and rejoice! Write about the change in your entire day because you were grateful for just being alive.

_____

_____

_____

_____

_____

_____

I am thankful for the people who are kind in traffic.

That's right. How caring is it when I want to make a left turn and someone kindly lets me go? I now take the opportunity to look them in the eyes and say *thank you* instead of a casual wave. Every opportunity is a gift, even a good parking space.

Kindness does happen to us every day. Don't be too busy to notice. Look back on your day and see what you can discover as a kind act missed. Then be grateful you remembered and write it down. Consider it a lesson to be more aware in the future.

_____

_____

_____

_____

_____

_____

I am thankful for my friends.

Friends have come and gone

throughout my life. Each one, for

whatever time they are a part of my

journey, gives me special gifts that,

perhaps unbeknownst to me, I need at

the time. Now I am better at

appreciating those gifts in the present.

Look for the gifts embedded in your relationships with your existing friends or ones from the past. What is it about their presence in your life that supported you? What have you been missing that now is clear? Even relationships that seem to end "badly" had an important message for you. Write about what you discover when you look a little deeper.

_____

_____

_____

_____

_____

I am thankful for the ability to vote.

I live in the United States of America where we have the right to have a say in what goes on. Regardless of political views, this right is not to be taken lightly. There are so many places in the world where people struggle to have this same opportunity. I believe you cannot complain unless you exert your right to vote!

So get out there and vote. If you are not registered, do so. If you know someone who needs a ride to a polling location, give them a ride. Ask your friends if they are registered. Speak out about the importance and privilege that we all have in this country. List what you have done, or can do, to forward the democratic process.

_____

_____

_____

_____

_____

I am thankful for clean water.

As of this writing 1.1 billion people in the world do not have safe drinking water. So when I sip away all day on water, I remember this is a precious commodity that I merely turn a faucet on to get.

The next time you go to your faucet, remember the many people who do not have that luxury. So don't waste it! The simplest of our pleasures in life are truly essentials that are missing from so many other human beings lives. Take a few moments to recognize an everyday occurrence in your life that might be extraordinary in someone else's. List them here.

_____

_____

_____

_____

_____

_____

I am thankful for the opportunity to LAUGH every day.

No matter what is going on in my day, I make time to laugh. It creates a healthy mind, body and spirit. It relieves stress, it heals my ills and it restores my faith in the direction I have chosen for my journey. Perhaps the best part of laughter is sharing it with others.

Go ahead. Take a deep breath and just laugh as hard as you can, for as long as you can. Repeat as necessary to change your perspective. Write about how that made you feel.

_____

_____

_____

_____

_____

I am thankful for people who allow me to share my love with them.

Love is a precious part of my soul. I give it freely, but not everyone is willing to take it. I continue to learn how to keep my love pure and free from attachment. Those who can accept it enrich my life through sharing, and those that struggle with it, teach me.

Think about those that allow you to share your love. Remember how special they are. If you have those who struggle with what you have to give, is the problem what you attach to your love or just a timing issue? Write about who you love and how they enrich your life. Write about the lessons you learn from those who love you as well.

_____

_____

_____

_____

_____

_____

I am thankful for the moments I take to learn about myself.

There is no telling how long my journey will be in this life. Every moment I deliberately find new information about myself, I create a world more suited to who I truly am.

There is no destination, no endgame, only a continuous band of time where I can continue to grow into the real me. It is my true self that I will be the most happy with.

When is the last time you really sat and listened to yourself? How long has it been since you took the time to hear your inner voice tell you what makes you truly happy? Take a moment to listen to your insightful self and learn one more aspect of what will make a happier you. Write it down here so you don't forget.

_____

_____

_____

_____

_____

*I am thankful for those who
share their experiences.*

It is so wonderful to be surrounded by

those who will keep me from

"reinventing the wheel." Their

experiences can give me a new

perspective on how to interact with

the world around me. To filter what is

useful to me and what does not fit who

I am or want to be is the secret of this

gift.

People are constantly sharing what
they have learned from their
experiences, many times without
being asked. This probably happens
every day. Make 3 columns to identify
what you have asked for, who gave of
themselves today and how it was
helpful. Always appreciate them by
saying thank you.

_____

_____

_____

_____

_____

_____

I am thankful for those who find it difficult to open up.

This is a great occasion for me to challenge myself. With great patience, continued kindness, and a smile, it is such a thrill to see the "curmudgeon" finally respond in a positive way. It is like the best present ever!

Do not dismiss those that are not able
to be as open as you might be.
Everyone has a story and most of the
time we have no idea what that is. So
who do you know that you have just
written off as a sourpuss? Make it
your mission to show them, by
example, how grand life can be.
Remember ... patience is a virtue.
Write down your plan here.

_____

_____

_____

_____

_____

*I am thankful for the
heartaches I have endured.*

Heartache gives me the occasion to

recognize what is truly important in

my life. Pain gives me a springboard

for the opportunities of joy. The art of

letting go gives me the ability to make

sure heartache is short-lived.

Forgiveness is truly a gift I give to

myself.

Embrace your heartache. Think of it as just another learning process. Practice forgiveness for the little stuff in life and you will be more proficient when it comes to those times in life that seem genuinely overwhelming. There truly is nothing that cannot be forgiven. Make a note as to what or who you want to forgive today.

_____

_____

_____

_____

_____

I am thankful for FINALLY getting a project done that has been lingering on for what seems like FOREVER!

I feel like I have climbed Mt. Kilimanjaro when I complete a task that has been hanging around like cement shoes on pool day. I am so happy with myself that I just stop what I am doing and perform a happy dance ... like Snoopy.

Everyone has these projects. They
seem like a good idea at the time and
you just can't let them go. ("No, I
really do need to put every picture I
have ever taken in the last 10 years
into an album!") So for those you hang
on to, break them down into little
pieces, celebrate each step of the way
and do your happy dance when you
are done. Jot down which one you are
going to tackle.

_____

_____

_____

_____

_____

_____

I am thankful for the ability to serve my community.

There are so many ways I serve my community and ultimately my world. It is worth my time to serve humanity. Giving to others has its own inherent rewards. I feel more of an integral part of all that surrounds me. This makes me happy!

Find a way to serve your fellow man. It can be large or small. It can be ongoing or a one shot deal. You may fancy reading to the blind, planting flowers along the highway, driving for Meals on Wheels, or helping in a school classroom. The opportunities abound. Find one that suits you and just do it! Write yourself a reminder about where you are going to help out and when.

_____

_____

_____

_____

_____

_____

I am thankful for the ability to change.

The greatest aspect of being a human being is that I have free will. I get to change whenever I want to. If I don't like how I acted a second ago, every moment I get to choose again. I find this so liberating. When I have acted in a manner that does not serve me or those around me, I can change me.

Delight in the gift of change. You
never have to continue behavior that
does not make your life harmonious.
Use this power at any moment to stop
and start again in a way that fills you
with joy. Become more aware of your
actions. What can you change in
yourself to be more aligned with your
preferred path in life? Take some time
to think about it, then write it down
here.

_____

_____

_____

_____

_____

I am thankful for what I do have in my life.

The simple treasures that make me rich are not tangible. It is my duty to focus on what I do have in my life as opposed to what I think I am missing. With a greater awareness of the gifts in my life, I can maintain my perspective of ABUNDANCE!

At the end of your day, do you tend to think about what you don't have? Do you spend your precious minutes thinking about what you desire? Take some time right now to list the simple but important gifts that you possess. Start with the fact that you are breathing.

_____

_____

_____

_____

_____

_____

*I am thankful that I notice
when people are kind to me.*

I notice when someone cares enough to

call and ask about my life. I notice

when someone takes the time to write

me a personal note of encouragement

or support. I notice when someone

readily helps me when I am in need. I

notice when somebody aids me when I

am *not* obviously in need. I notice a

smile from a stranger.

When you have major issues going on in your life, it is easier to notice those who help in BIG ways. But what about the ways in which the world around you reaches out in various kind ways every day? It takes a deliberate effort to get in the habit of recognizing this kindness when it occurs. Is there something you missed lately? Think deeply and write down your discoveries. And remember to let those people know you appreciate their kindness.

_____

_____

_____

_____

_____

I am thankful for the gift of gab.

My passion is to teach others through presentations. Yes I prepare and I practice, but I have certainly been given a gift in the ease in which I can fulfill this dream. Some parts of me are inherent and I am grateful to have found them and made use of their inspirational powers.

Each of you has intrinsic gifts that allow you to have special talents in your lives. These are the essential parts of you that will allow you to find true happiness. Write about your special talents that give you great joy.

_____

_____

_____

_____

_____

_____

I am thankful for LOVE!

I cherish the love of my family. I treasure the love of my friends. I don't discount the love of my dog. Each day I work on remembering that I also want to continue to love myself. I strive to live my life in a way that is worthy of loving me.

Who loves you? Count each one as a blessing every day. You can never appreciate the love of another human being too much. It is a very special gift. However, the love of yourself is the one love that will truly make you happy. What do you love about yourself? Continue to add to this list.

_____

_____

_____

_____

_____

_____

I am thankful for the power of forgiveness.

Forgiveness is truly about letting go of the past. In forgiving others, I accept who they are. In forgiving myself, I accept my failings and learn to love myself again. The gift of forgiveness is truly liberating!

All things can be forgiven. This can
only be accomplished when you have
learned that forgiveness does not
mean agreeing with a certain
behavior, it means accepting ...
without judgments. Write down who
you can forgive when you finally don't
judge their behavior.

_____

_____

_____

_____

_____

I am thankful for my health.

Being healthy is an enhancement to life. I am proud that I watch what I eat, keep my body moving, make sure my mind is enriched and keep my spiritual self-enlightened. It is work I enjoy because the rewards allow me to feel *awakened*.

Being healthy is more than just not having a cold. Your body has many degrees of being healthy and it is up to you to recognize and appreciate what is working well, even when other parts may be in turmoil. An open mind and an open heart touch your very soul and directly affect staying healthy in your body. List the many ways in which you are healthy.

_____

_____

_____

_____

_____

*I am thankful for the
prospect of learning another
life lesson.*

It takes continual self-awareness for

me to stay on the path of learning. The

keener my senses, the more I absorb,

the more distracted I can become.

When, however, I slow down enough to

appreciate all that is my life, I can be

open to learn something new about

myself and the world around me. New

life lessons magnify all that I have.

Take some time every day to slow down enough to really notice what is going on in your life. It may be your own actions in word or deed. It may be the behavior of another human or nature. There is always something to learn. Write about what life lesson you were aware of today.

_____

_____

_____

_____

_____

_____

I am thankful for the opportunity of Surprise!

When I least expect it ... WHAM! If I have been living under the guise of "knowing it all," surprises happen much more often. This is a good reminder to live in the present. Without the illusion of control, I can actually enjoy the element of surprise and rejoice in its wonder. Now that is something to be thankful for.

Be aware. What surprised you lately? What were you really not expecting? A compliment? A green light? A call or letter from a friend? Once you understand how wonderful a surprise can be, you might choose to be that bright surprise to someone else. Write about a surprise you took the time to notice that filled you with joy. Or, write about what you are planning to do that will delight someone you know.

I am thankful when I keep myself in the present.

Yesterday is gone and I can never

change it. Tomorrow is an unknown

and, no matter how I try and figure it

out, it will be different when I get

there. All I really have is "now" and it

is perfect. It is perfect because it is

what I have. Each second it changes.

It takes a lot of practice to stay in the "now." It is only then that you can truly enjoy what is going on in your life at the moment. Practice writing what is occurring right now in your life. Then look back days later and you will understand how time changes your perspective. Write about what you think might happen in the future and then look back when you get to that juncture and see how different it is. These types of practices help to show you the value of appreciating life in each of its precious moments.

_____

_____

_____

More space for exploration on next page.

I'm thankful for ...

"Yesterday is gone.

Tomorrow has not

yet come.

We have only today.

Let us begin."

Mother Theresa

About the Author

Julie Ann Sullivan works with organizations who want to create a work environment where people are productive, engaged and appreciated.

Julie Ann Sullivan speaks from experience. Many people consider her "a revolutionary." She does not shy away from that title! She believes when people are given a new way of thinking they have a better attitude towards work and life. Julie Ann seeks to bring a more positive and productive environment into every business she visits. She is an author and a professional member of the National Speakers Association.

Julie Ann's programs are high in content infused with a measure of humor and motivation.

Visit Julie Ann's website @
http://www.JulieAnnSullivan.com

Now What?

Schedule Julie Ann for your next event,
conference or training by calling direct to
724-942-0486, or email her at
julieann@julieannsullivan.com.

All presentations are tailored exclusively for
your audience.

Julie Ann can accommodate audiences from
10 to 10,000.

Quotes about Gratitude

"For Gratitude to flourish, it needs to be
shared"
Julie Ann Sullivan

"No one who achieves success does so
without acknowledging the help of others."
Alfred North Whitehead

"Joy is the simplest form of gratitude."
Karl Barth

GET CREATIVE!

Made in the USA
Middletown, DE
01 May 2021